AnimalWays

Dogs

AnimalWays

Dogs

Rebecca Stefoff

Benchmark Books
MARSHALL CAVENDISH
NEW YORK

In memory of the Stefoff family dogs, Poncho and Lassie

With thanks to Dr. Dan Wharton, director of the Central Park Wildlife Center, for his expert reading of this manuscript.

Benchmark Books
Marshall Cavendish
99 White Plains Road
Tarrytown, NY 10591-9001
Website: www.marshallcavendish.com

Library of Congress Cataloging-in-Publication Data
Stefoff, Rebecca, 1951–
Dogs / by Rebecca Stefoff.
p. cm. — (AnimalWays)
Includes bibliographical references and index.
Summary: Describes the evolution, body structure, and behavior of dogs, and discusses their interaction with people.
Contents: Dogs and people—How dogs developed—The biology of the dog—Canine behavior—The life cycle—A world of dogs.
ISBN 0-7614-1393-6
1. Dogs—Juvenile literature. [1. Dogs.] I. Title. II. Animalways.
SF426.5 .S724   2002   636.7—dc21   2002001530

Photo Research by Candlepants Incorporated

Cover Photo: Animals Animals/J & P Wegner

The photographs in this book are used by permission and through the courtesy of: *Photo Researchers Inc.*: Elizabeth Lemoine, 2; Jeff Lapore, 13; E. Vogeler/Okapia, 20–21; Sylvain Cordier, 26; Jeanne White, 38 (middle), 55, 67; Renne Lynn, 38 (lower), 39 (top left), 39 (lower right), 77; Richard Hutchings, 43, 68; John Kaprielian, 46, 52, 70; Carolyn A. McKeone, 61; Tom & Pat Leeson, 63; Alan & Sandy Carey, 65, 87; Explorer, 74; Margaret Miller, 81; Barbara Young, 84–85; Terry Whitaker, 95; Gregory G. Dimijian, 96; Info Hund/Kramer/okapia, 100–101; Blair Seitz, 102; Tim Davis, back cover; *Corbis*: Michael S. Lewis, 9; Charles & Josette Lenars, 18; Archivo iconographica S.A., 19; Bettman, 27; Layne Kennedy, 31; Kennen Ward, 33 (left); John Conrad 33 (right); Dale S. Spartas, 38 (top); Cordaiy Photo Library Ltd., 47, 58; Robert Dowling, 53; Tim Page, 93; Wolfgang Kaehler, 98; Tom Nebbia, 103. *Erich Lessing/Art Resource, NY*: 24; *Animals/Animals*: B. Osborne 29; Robert Pearcy, 39 (top right), 91; Ralph Reinhold, 39 (lower left); Robert Maier, 40; Renee Stockdale, 56; Michael Habicht, 72; Gerard Lacz, 80; Leonard L.T. Rhodes, 88.

Printed in Italy

1 3 5 6 4 2

Contents

Animal Kingdom

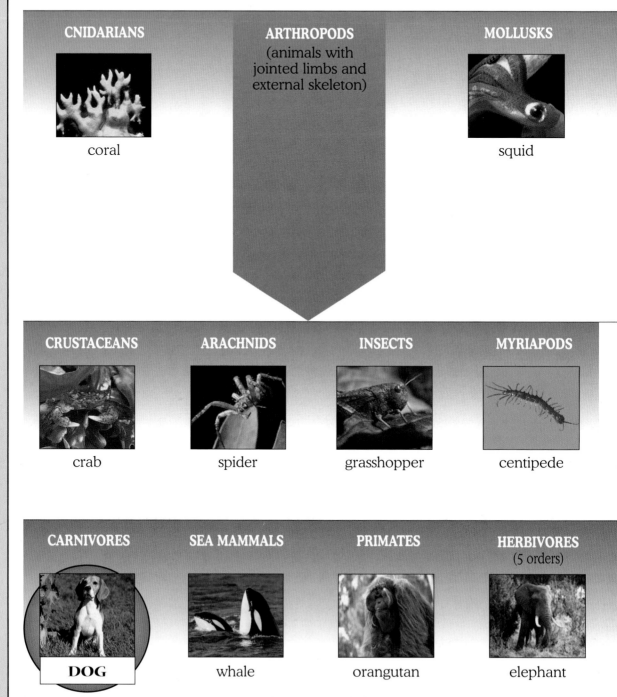

CNIDARIANS

coral

ARTHROPODS
(animals with jointed limbs and external skeleton)

MOLLUSKS

squid

CRUSTACEANS

crab

ARACHNIDS

spider

INSECTS

grasshopper

MYRIAPODS

centipede

CARNIVORES

DOG

SEA MAMMALS

whale

PRIMATES

orangutan

HERBIVORES
(5 orders)

elephant

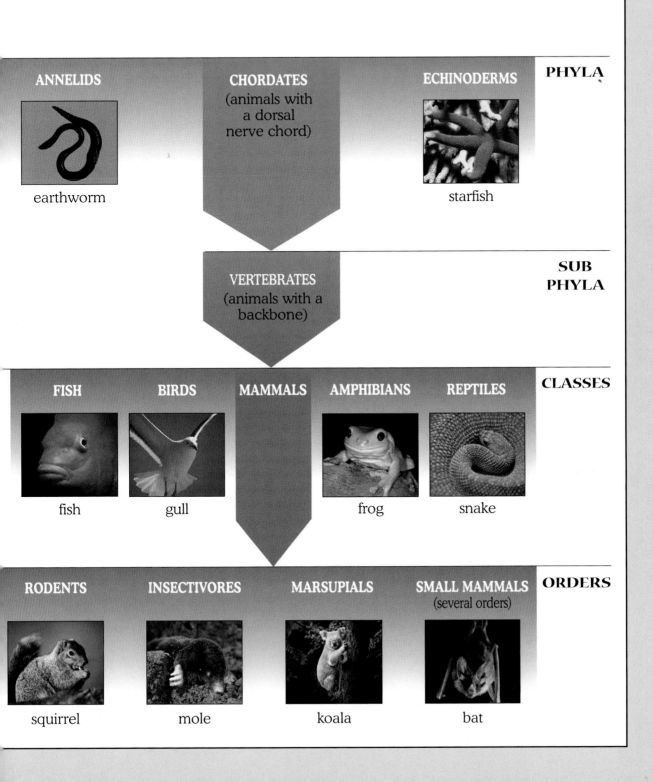

PHYLA

ANNELIDS

earthworm

CHORDATES
(animals with
a dorsal
nerve chord)

ECHINODERMS

starfish

**SUB
PHYLA**

VERTEBRATES
(animals with a
backbone)

CLASSES

FISH

fish

BIRDS

gull

MAMMALS

AMPHIBIANS

frog

REPTILES

snake

ORDERS

RODENTS

squirrel

INSECTIVORES

mole

MARSUPIALS

koala

SMALL MAMMALS
(several orders)

bat

1 Dogs and People

In 1808 the British poet Lord Byron wrote these words for a monument to mark the grave of a beloved friend: "Near this spot are deposited the remains of one who possessed beauty without vanity, strength without insolence, courage without ferocity, and all the virtues of Man, without his vices. This praise, which would be unmeaning flattery if inscribed over human ashes, is but a just tribute to the memory of Boatswain, a dog." A century and a half later the American writer John Steinbeck, author of a famous and comical account of travels with a poodle named Charley, wrote that the qualities people most admire in dogs—such as loyalty and bravery—are the qualities they wish for in themselves.

Throughout the ages, people around the world have treasured tales of noble, heroic dogs. Many works of art and literature celebrate the animal that has been called "man's best friend." It's not surprising that dogs have won the hearts of so many

LIKE THIS COLORADO FARMER, PEOPLE AROUND THE WORLD COUNT ON THEIR DOGS FOR COMPANIONSHIP AND FOR SERVICES SUCH AS HERDING AND GUARDING.

people. Dogs were the first animals to live with humans, and over thousands of years humans have tailored their canine companions to meet their needs. Nature gave the dog's ancestors certain characteristics that made it a good partner, but people made dogs into the animals they are today.

First to Be Tamed

Like all animals that live with humans or under their control, dogs had to be domesticated, or tamed. Many mysteries surround the domestication of dogs, but one of the biggest mysteries has been solved. Scientists had long known that dogs are part of the Canidae, the family of doglike animals that also includes wolves, foxes, jackals, coyotes, and all wild dogs. But precisely where did dogs fit in? For years scientists debated whether the many modern breeds, or varieties, of domestic dog were descended from wild dogs, wolves, or jackals, or perhaps from all three. More recently, however, the majority of researchers have agreed that all modern domestic dogs, from the tiniest, fluffiest Pekingese to the largest, sleekest greyhound, are descendents of wolves. However, some experts think the ancestral subspecies or strain of wolves from which dogs descended is now extinct.

Knowing that today's dogs came from wolf ancestors, though, raises more questions. Exactly how did the wild ancestral wolf turn into the tame dog? When and where did it happen? And how did dogs develop into the many quite different breeds that we know today? Although some questions may never be fully answered, scientists from many fields are now studying the long relationship between humans and dogs. Biologists and paleontologists, for example, examine the physical links between the canids for information about how wolves and dogs evolved, or changed over time. Ethologists, who are students of animal behavior, observe wolves for clues as to how such creatures might have become domesticated in the distant past. They also study the wolflike traits of dogs. Archaeologists study the traces left by past human societies, and sometimes, when sifting through the dust of long-ago settlements, they find the remains of canids. Such finds can help pinpoint the earliest appearances of dogs. Finally, anthropologists, who study human cultures, gather information about how dogs and people have interacted over the years and about the roles that dogs have filled in human history.

Most experts believe that people had dogs before they had donkeys, horses, sheep, goats, cattle, cats, or chickens. But although researchers agree that dogs were the first animals to be tamed, there is less agreement about when, where, and how their domestication took place. By the time humans began keeping records of their own history, dogs were already part of that history. Those interested in the puzzle of canine origins must look further back in time and rely on indirect evidence, such as bones found in the ancient burial sites and refuse dumps that mark the places where prehistoric people once lived.

A picture of dog origins began to develop in the 1980s, when genetic research opened the way to a clearer understanding of the relationships among various kinds of animals. This research confirmed that modern dogs and wolves share a wolf ancestor, as many people had long believed. A theory about the origin of dogs took shape. This theory holds that wolves and prehistoric people lived near each other in many parts of the ancient world. These people probably hunted wolves from time to time. A glacial period began more than 20,000 years ago and lasted until about 11,000 years ago, bringing snow, ice, and low temperatures to the northern part of the world. During this time people in northern Europe and Asia needed warm furs to wear, and so the hunting of wolves for their furs increased. Sometimes a mother wolf was killed, leaving young pups. Drawn to the cute appearance and playful ways of the orphan pups, people adopted them and cared for them— just as people sometimes do today.

Wolves are adapted to live in groups called packs, with a clear-cut order of leaders and followers. For this reason, the young adopted wolves fit well into their human communities. They regarded the humans who took care of them as their pack mates and pack leaders. Their behavior was more orderly and predictable than that of most wild animals, so people let them stay—probably killing those whose behavior was too wild and occasionally adding new pups that had "tame" qualities. People learned that the canids living among them made good hunting partners and guards because wolves in the wild hunt together and protect their packs and territories. As a result, the animals had value to their human owners, who learned to "improve" them by interbreeding the animals that had traits they liked, such as loyalty, obedience, and easiness to train. In this way, humans strengthened the qualities that they found useful or desirable. As canid generation followed generation, the animals grew ever tamer and easier to train. At some point, perhaps after hundreds of thousands of years, those canids had become different enough from wolves to be considered a new animal: the dog.

The raising of adopted wolf pups probably happened more than once, and maybe many times, in various parts of Asia and Europe. Migrating groups of people took their domesticated canids into Africa and North America. Many different dog populations developed around the globe. Features such as size and color differed somewhat from group to group because the groups were descended from different regional varieties of wolves. These differences grew greater as people began to breed

THE ANCESTORS OF DOGS WERE WOLVES THAT PROBABLY LOOKED MUCH LIKE THESE GRAY WOLVES. OVER TIME, DOGS EVOLVED INTO THE GREAT VARIETY OF BREEDS THAT EXIST TODAY.

different varieties of dogs for different uses: small dogs for house pets, fast dogs for chasing game such as rabbits, massive and strong dogs for guard duty, thick-haired dogs for life in cold climates, and so on. Eventually dogs became highly varied in appearance and widely distributed throughout most of the world.

Many biologists and experts in dog behavior share their theory that humans turned wild wolves into trainable dogs through selective breeding of wolves with "tame" traits. A few investigators, however, have other ideas. One of them is Raymond Coppinger, a biologist who has studied canines around the world. He offers the theory that dogs "domesticated" themselves through natural selection rather than through artificial selection by humans. Coppinger thinks that what people did to turn wolves into dogs was not to adopt pups but to create a new habitat, or ecological niche, in the world. When humans began living together in permanent settlements, the wastes they produced began to build up around these villages. In other words, the town dump is as old as the town. Gnawed bones, fish heads, discarded food, and other garbage attracted birds and animals to the village to scavenge for scraps.

Wolves were among the scavengers. Those wolves that were quick, adaptable, not too shy of people, and smaller and less ferocious than others succeeded best at taking advantage of the new food source. They moved easily around human settlements, They were less frightening to people than larger, wilder wolves, and they were less likely to attack people and be attacked in return. According to this view, these wolves were more likely to hang around villages and to be tolerated by the people who lived there. In wild wolf packs, these animals would probably not have produced offspring, for only the lead wolf in a pack mates with the females. But living on the fringes of human society, on the edges of villages, dumps, and fields, these wolves bred with each other, producing new generations that were more and more tame and comfortable around people. In this way, dogs evolved naturally from their wild ancestors. And when people saw the value of the semidomestic canids who cleaned up their garbage and destroyed rats and other vermin, they began adopting and training them, eventually breeding them for special purposes.

Scientists may never be able to determine which of these theories is correct. Perhaps dogs entered human communities as both adopted pups *and* tolerated scavengers, or perhaps some completely different method of domestication occurred. But however the destinies of dogs and humans became joined, dogs are now an important part of human life and culture.

Dogs in Early History

The shift from wolf to dog happened so gradually that no one could point to a particular animal (or its bones) and say, "Here is the first dog." Still, scientists are working on pinning down the general age of the dog—for example, a 1997 article in the journal *Science* claimed that dogs originated as early as 135,000 years ago. Many experts have argued that the evidence presented for that claim does not stand up to close examination, and the general view is that dogs originated much more recently, perhaps around 15,000 years ago. By about 12,000 years ago, many researchers agree, dogs seem to have been present in at least some human communities.

Two 12,000-year-old fossil finds from Israel hint at the existence of dogs in a very early village there. One find is the tooth of a small but full-grown canid found where a house once stood. The other is a burial site containing the bones of a woman together with those of a puppy. Both the tooth and the puppy skeleton could have belonged to either a dog or a wolf. But some researchers think that because they were found in human settlements, they are likely to be the remains of domestic canids—animals that were either dogs or very close to becoming dogs. The same is true of other canid fossils found in settlements dating from 10,000 to 12,000 years ago. It is impossible to know for certain whether they came from wolves or dogs, but they suggest that domestic canids were becoming increasingly common.

Around 8,000 years ago animals recognizable as dogs began to appear in the art—and later in the writings—of ancient cultures. Some of the oldest known images of dogs are found on pieces of broken pottery from the region once known as Mesopotamia (now the nation of Iraq), which was home to the ancient civilizations of Sumer, Assyria, and Babylonia. The first dogs to be pictured look much like modern greyhounds. These lean, sleek, long-legged dogs are shown hunting fast-moving gazelles. Soon after another kind of dog appeared: a large-headed, thick-necked, strong animal belonging to what is now called the mastiff family of dogs. The ruins of the palace of King Assurbanipal in the Assyrian capital of Nineveh, built in 649 B.C., have wall carvings of mastiffs on leashes, walking at the sides of their owners. People used mastiffs to hunt fierce prey such as lions and wild boars and to guard important buildings such as temples and palaces. Mastiffs could be trained as combat dogs and often accompanied armies into battles. Prisoners were sometimes executed by being fed alive to mastiffs kept half-starved for that purpose.

A third type of dog lived in Mesopotamia and elsewhere in the ancient world. Often called the village dog, it was a lean, quick scavenger that resembled a small wolf or modern coyote.

People tolerated these dogs but do not seem to have bred, tended, trained, or housed them. Instead these semi-wild animals lived in streets and dumps, surviving on the refuse of human societies much as their wild ancestors might have done. Some cultures regarded village dogs with disgust, perhaps because they occasionally ate corpses and carried disease, or parasites such as tapeworms. Similar dogs—ownerless, half-wild scavengers—still live in villages and town dumps in many parts of the world. In India they are called pariah dogs, and the word pariah has come to mean "outcast." Many societies see a great difference between the dogs that they breed and raise for their own purposes, which are well regarded, and the pariah or scavenger dogs, which are viewed with distaste and kept at a distance.

The ancient Egyptians had domestic dogs that they greatly valued. Paintings on the walls of tombs dating from as early as 2500 B.C. show various sizes and types of dogs wearing collars and leashes. Dogs apparently served the Egyptians in battle, in the hunt, as guardians of property, and as family pets. After death, many dogs received the same treatment that people did: They were mummified, or treated with chemicals and wrapped in strips of linen to preserve their bodies. Special cemeteries were set aside for dogs in many towns. Modern archaeologists have unearthed many hundreds of dogs laid to rest in this way.

The ancient Greeks had hunting and guard dogs. Among these were mastiffs, brought into Greece from Persia (modern Iran) and Mesopotamia. The Romans used dogs for cattle herding and hunting. They also had fights pitting them against each other or against wild beasts. Dogs in the Roman army not only attacked enemy soldiers but also carried messages. Romans also valued dogs for defense, and ordinary civilians often kept watchdogs in their homes. In Pompeii, a Roman city buried by

THE ANCIENT EGYPTIANS
FILLED THEIR TOMBS
WITH IMAGES OF THINGS
THEY THOUGHT THEY
WOULD NEED IN THE
AFTERLIFE. STATUES OF
DOGS WERE OFTEN
BURIED WITH THE DEAD.
THIS CANINE SCULPTURE
CAME FROM THE TOMB
OF KING TUTANKHAMEN,
WHO DIED AROUND
1322 B.C.

a volcanic eruption and rediscovered in modern times, the entrances of many houses feature images of dogs with the words *Cave canem*, Latin for "Beware of the dog." By the time of the Romans, dogs had developed into a number of distinct types, the forerunners of the modern breeds. In addition to mastiffs and greyhounds, the Romans had bloodhounds, sheepdogs, and small house pets they called lapdogs. Some of these pampered pets had jeweled collars and elaborate doghouses.

Several types of dog developed in Asia. Many authorities think that the mastiff originated in Tibet or central Asia and was carried westward into Persia and Mesopotamia by migrating tribes. In time the Tibetans came to have three general types of dog: village dogs or pariahs, large mastiffs used as guard dogs and

ROMAN ARTWORK FROM THE SECOND CENTURY A.D. SHOWS A HUNTER AND HIS DOGS.

herd dogs, and small, long-haired dogs that were pets in house-holds and monasteries. These small Tibetan dogs eventually gave rise to the breeds now known as Lhasa apso and shih tzu. Starting around A.D. 1600, shih tzus were taken to China, where they became known as "lion-dogs." Kept inside temples and

palaces, they barked warnings when intruders entered. A breed called the shar-pei, noted for its baggy skin, had emerged in central China by about A.D. 220, probably as a result of the special breeding of mastiffs and other herding and hunting dogs. Chinese emperors and aristocrats also created another breed of small lion-dog noted for its short noses and long, silky fur—the Pekingese, named for Peking, as the Chinese capital city Beijing used to be called. These small, valuable dogs were imperial property, and anyone caught smuggling one out of the palace risked torture. Still, the dogs eventually found their way into general Chinese society and even, through trade, into the hands of European dog fanciers. Farther north, people in Siberia and northern China and Japan had strong, large-bodied dogs with thick, bushy hair and upcurled tails.

Wolves and dogs migrated into the Americas the same way people probably did, by crossing the land bridge that linked northeastern Siberia to western Alaska during the Ice Age, when the level of the world's oceans was much lower than it is today. In the Americas, various societies used dogs for hunting, guard duty, and transport. Native Americans had no horses until after the arrival of the Europeans around A.D. 1500, but

THE PEKINGESE ORIGINATED IN CHINA, WHERE IT WAS CALLED A "LION-DOG." THESE DOGS WERE SO PRECIOUS THAT ONLY THE IMPERIAL FAMILY COULD POSSESS THEM.

their dogs pulled vehicles such as the sled and the travois, a framework of poles and skins used for hauling goods. Some cultures in North, Central, and South America also raised dogs for food, as did some Asians. The Aztec people of Mexico sacrificed dogs to their gods during religious rituals. They created the very small type of dog known today as the Chihuahua.

The Romans carried dogs throughout Europe. When the Roman Empire collapsed, and with it the Romans' tightly run settlements, European dogs became somewhat wild again. Large numbers of them took to living in forests and fields, preying on livestock and even peasants. For centuries most Europeans feared and disliked dogs. Not until about the year A.D. 1000 did they begin to prize and carefully breed once again. By then, Europeans had begun to create a culture of nobility, and nobles took much pleasure in the hunt. Fine hunting dogs became valuable possessions. Various pointers, greyhounds, hounds, mastiffs, and terriers tracked, located, chased, and brought down game birds and animals. In *A Treatise on Hunting*, a French nobleman of the fourteenth century wrote about the breeding and care of dogs. The author was said to travel everywhere with 1,600 hunting dogs of his own.

Within a few hundred years dogs were appearing in portraits with their royal or noble owners. These animals were usually prized hunting greyhounds for the men and well-groomed lap dogs, or miniatures, for the women. Ordinary European shopkeepers and farmers also had dogs of their own, generally mastiffs or mongrels, as dogs of mixed or uncertain breed are sometimes called. By the eighteenth century, dogs were commonly kept as household and family pets, not just workers, hunters, or watchdogs. The first dog show took place in Great Britain in 1859. Many others soon followed, proving that dogs had become extremely popular with large numbers of people.

From its humble beginnings as a scavenger or orphan pup, the dog had taken its place as a partner, servant, companion, and beloved friend of humankind.

Dogs in Legend and Lore

Dogs occupy a special place in the world. They are not the only animals to live with or be controlled by people, but unlike such domesticated animals as the cow and the sheep, dogs are hunters and carnivores. Domestic cats are hunters, too, but they are small, while many dogs are large and capable of being quite fierce. Dogs are a link between the domestic and the wild. They are tame, familiar, and often amazingly loyal. But they are also a living link to those dangerous creatures whose eyes gleamed in the darkness beyond our own ancestors' flickering firelight.

In myths and stories people have used dogs to represent both the dangers of the savage animal world and the virtues of the orderly human world. Some Greek myths reflect dogs' fierceness. Cerberus, for example, was a monstrous three-headed dog said to guard the entrance to the underworld, and Actaeon was a hunter who was devoured by his own dogs as punishment after he glimpsed the goddess Artemis while she was bathing. Other Greek legends dwell on canine cleverness and courage. Dogs that guarded temples were rumored to be able to tell the difference between Greeks and non-Greeks and to keep the foreigners from entering. Another legend says that during a war the Greek city of Corinth was guarded by fifty mastiffs. Invaders killed forty-nine of them, but the fiftieth dog fought free and roused the city's defenders, who later rewarded their canine savior with a silver collar. And the Greek epic poem *The Odyssey* contains one of the earliest of many stories about a dog's keen senses and loyal heart—when the hero Odysseus returns home

after years of wandering, the only one who recognizes him is his faithful old dog, Argos.

The close relationship between humans and dogs becomes even closer in some myths. Traditions in Siberia and other parts of the northern world say that the ancestors of the first people were dogs, or were nourished by the milk of mother dogs. One

Siberian legend says that people were created before dogs. When the first human being died, all the others wept and grieved. The Creator sent a dog to Earth to tell people how to bring the dead back to life. But the dog became confused and instead showed the people how to bury their dead.

In Central Africa people traditionally regarded the basenji, an African breed of dog, as the bringer of fire and civilization to people. Legend says that the dog once guarded the fire of the gods, but a man wanted some fire and promised to take care of the dog forever if the dog would steal some fire and bring it to him. The dog did so, and man and dog have lived together ever since. Other legends from Africa and elsewhere in the world say that dogs' breath and saliva have the power to cure illness in humans. Some traditional folk medicine includes dog parts. In southern Africa, for example, folk healers sometimes grind the bones of the oldest dog in the village into a medicine that is supposed to give long life.

Many dog breeds have their own particular legends. The little lion dogs of China, bred by the emperors and their families and servants, were said to represent Guatama Buddha, the founder of the Buddhist religion, and to have the power of making themselves as large as lions. Arabians believed that their salukis—swift dogs with plumed tails, once used in the hunting of gazelles—were gifts from Allah, or God. Traditionally, while they regarded other dogs as unclean, they praised the saluki's speed in stories and sayings such as, "My saluki will catch a gazelle and bring him down even if that gazelle should spring up to the stars and vault over the moon." The dalmatian, a spotted, short-haired dog that in modern times has been associated with fire stations, is said to have appeared in a dream centuries ago to a woman whose son became Saint Dominic, the founder of the Catholic religious order called the Dominicans. In her dream a

LEAN, GRACEFUL, AND FAST, SALUKIS BECAME THE STUFF OF POETRY IN ARABIA, WHERE THEY WERE USED AS HUNTING DOGS.

black-and-white dog carried a torch with which to burn witches and unbelievers. Her son's religious order, inspired by the dream, wore black-and-white garments and used the image of the dog in its art. Its members were called the *Domini canes*, "hounds of God" in Latin.

Modern popular culture has produced many memorable and endearing dogs, including Lassie, Rin Tin Tin, Buck in Jack London's *Call of the Wild*, Old Yeller, Lady and the Tramp, the *101 Dalmations*, and Beethoven. Like old legends, these new stories give people something they love—tales of dogs who are sometimes comical yet also brave, intelligent, and capable of outwitting villains and saving their owners. Countless cartoons, jokes, and stories give dogs the standard canine name Fido. Although not everyone today realizes it, that name points to the quality people prize above all in their canine friends. It comes from the Latin *fidelis* and means "faithful" or "loyal."

THE CANINE HERO OF THE TELEVISION SERIES *RIN TIN TIN*, WHICH RAN IN THE UNITED STATES FROM 1954 THROUGH 1959, WAS AN ALERT, BRAVE, AND INTELLIGENT GERMAN SHEPHERD.

2

How Dogs Developed

Dogs are fairly new arrivals on Earth, but the family they belong to has been around for millions of years. Using the evidence of fossil bones, piecing together scattered clues such as teeth and skull fragments, paleontologists have traced the ancestry of dogs and their relatives far back in time. The story of how dogs evolved is largely the story of how wolves evolved, and that story is not completely clear. Scientists are still sorting out the details. But they have learned enough to give us a general idea of how wolves originated. Their family tree took root not long after the age of the dinosaurs.

Canine Origins

Dogs belong to the large group of animals known as carnivores,

ALTHOUGH THESE HUSKIES RESEMBLE WOLVES IN APPEARANCE, THEY ARE NO CLOSER TO WOLVES, IN TERMS OF DESCENT OR GENETICS, THAN ANY OTHER SPECIES OF DOG.

or meat eaters. Until 65 million years ago the most successful carnivores on the planet were dinosaurs. When the dinosaurs became extinct, the small mammals that had shared their world began to occupy more roles and habitats. Among those mammals was a group of small, weasel-like hunters called the miacids. Their teeth were very much like those of modern meat-eating animals. In particular, the miacids had the kind of tooth that scientists call a carnassial—a large rear tooth used for cutting meat. Scientists believe that all the carnivorous mammals in the world today descended from the miacids.

By about 55 million years ago the miacids were evolving into two general groups of carnivores. Scientists call one group aeluroids, from the Latin word for "catlike," and the other arctoids, which means "bearlike." The arctoid group contained the ancestors of both bears and dogs, as well as the ancestors of weasels, skunks, raccoons, sea lions, and otters. Arctoids had a plantigrade stride, which means that they walked with the soles of their feet flat on the ground, as bears do today.

Over time a number of different arctoid families evolved. One of those families, now called the Canidae, appeared about 35 million years ago. The earliest known members of the Canidae family were long-bodied animals with long muzzles, or snouts, and long tails that hung down toward the ground. Their legs were fairly short and their bodies were low-slung, closer to the ground than those of modern canids. These first canids differed from earlier arctoids in an important way. Instead of walking with a plantigrade stride, they had a digitigrade stride, which means that they walked on their toes. As they evolved, it appears, their foot bones gradually moved upward, until they occupied the positions taken by the ankle and shin bones of other animals. The paws on which they walked consisted of what had once been only their toes. This new structure and stride let

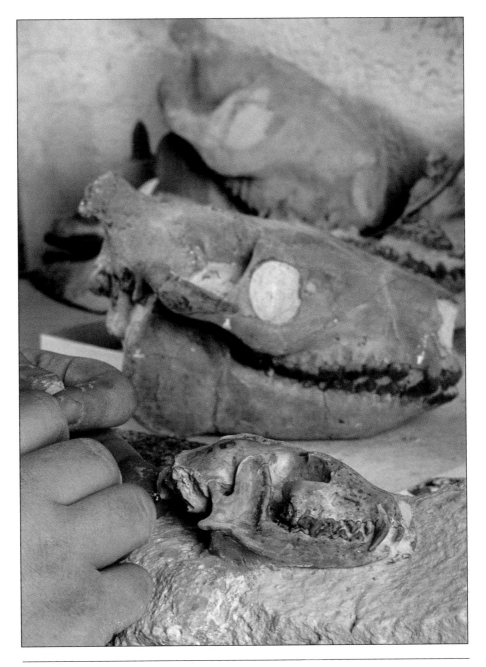

In the foreground is the fossil skull of a small early canid of the Oligocene period, from 37 to 24 million years ago. It was found in the Black Hills of South Dakota.

the Canidae run swiftly and maneuver nimbly, making them good predators, or hunters of other animals.

An early canid called *Cynodictis* was widespread in Europe and North America. The European version became extinct without leaving any descendents, but the North American animal was the ancestor of all later canids. *Tomarctus*, a descendant of *Cynodictis*, lived in North America 24 million years ago. About 12 million years ago some descendants of *Tomarctus* evolved into the genus *Canis*, a subgroup of the Canidae that includes wolves, jackals, and coyotes. (Foxes and other "wild dogs" are descended from other genera, or subgroups, of the Canidae family.)

Some paleontologists think that by about one million years ago the members of the wolf group had evolved into forms very similar to those of modern wolves. The animal that we know today as *Canis lupus*, the gray wolf, probably appeared some 300,000 years ago, or earlier, and spread through North America, Europe, and Asia. In different regions, subspecies of *Canis lupus* emerged. These included the small, short-haired Indian, or Asian, wolf and the large, bushy-haired timber, or northern, wolf. And somewhere, somehow, one or more of these subspecies of *Canis lupus* gave rise to dogs.

Dogs and Their Relatives

Like all plants and animals, the dog has a Latin scientific name. The name is part of a classification system called taxonomy, which organizes living things into groups by the characteristics they share. Taxonomy begins with large groups and proceeds through a series of categories, each smaller and more limited than the last. In this system the dog belongs to the kingdom Animalia (all animals), the phylum Chordata (all animals with spinal cords), the class Mammalia (all animals with backbones

SEVERAL SPECIES OF MODERN
CANIDS ARE CALLED WILD DOGS,
ALTHOUGH THEY DO NOT BELONG
TO THE GENUS THAT INCLUDES
WOLVES, JACKALS, COYOTES, AND
DOMESTIC DOGS. SUCH CANIDS,
INCLUDING THIS *LYCAON PICTUS*
FROM AFRICA, CANNOT INTER-
BREED WITH DOGS.

THE GRAY WOLF IS A CLEARLY
RECOGNIZED SPECIES. SCIENTISTS
DO NOT AGREE, HOWEVER, ON
WHETHER DOGS ARE A SUBGROUP
OF THE GRAY WOLF SPECIES OR A
SEPARATE SPECIES DESCENDED
FROM WOLVES.

that are mammals), the order Carnivora (all mammals that are carnivores), and the family Canidae (all canids, including wolves, foxes, jackals, coyotes, and wild and domestic dogs).

Canid classification is complicated beyond this point—in fact, it is one of the most hotly debated areas of mammal taxonomy. The classification of dogs and other canids has changed much in recent years, and it continues to change as new discoveries and new theories emerge. Not all scientists agree with the changes. In particular, the taxonomy of dogs is the starting point for discussions about how to define a species. This issue is important because the species has long been regarded as the basic unit of life. The notion of the species underlies everything from the teaching of biology to environmental-protection laws and programs.

For several hundred years scientists gave dogs the taxonomic label *Canis familiaris*, sometimes abbreviated to *C. familiaris*. This meant that dogs belonged to the genus *Canis*, just as the wolf did, but were considered a distinct species. Then, in 1982, a group of experts produced a new survey of the world's mammal species. They suggested that dogs be given a new scientific name, *Canis lupus familiaris*, which identifies dogs as a subspecies of the gray wolf, and not as a separate species. It puts the dog on the same taxonomic footing as *Canis lupus baileyi*, the Mexican gray wolf, or *Canis lupus pallipes*, the Asian wolf.

The dog's name change was part of a revision of the entire scheme of canid taxonomy. According to most recent versions of that scheme, the family of Canidae consists of more than thirty living species. Those species are divided into three subfamilies. One of those subfamilies is the Caninae. The subfamily of Caninae is, in turn, divided into four genera. One of the four is the genus *Canis*, which includes seven species: the gray wolf, the red wolf of North America, the coyote (sometimes called the prairie wolf), and four species of jackals found in Asia and Africa. The domestic dog sprang from one member of this genus, and the others are its closest relatives. Dogs can interbreed with the other species in the genus *Canis*.

Many scientific and conservation groups, including the Smithsonian Institution and the World Conservation Union, have accepted the classification of the dog as *C. lupus familiaris*, a type of wolf. Not all scientists, however, find the new label helpful or even meaningful. Raymond Coppinger defines species from the viewpoint of an ecologist, a scientist interested in how organisms interact with their environment. To an ecologist, a species is an animal that is adapted to occupy a particular niche, a role or place in an environment. No other animal fits exactly into that niche.

"As a behavioral ecologist," writes Coppinger, "I regard the dog, *Canis familiaris*, as a separate species, a product of a distinct evolutionary event. The dog is beautifully adapted . . . to feed and reproduce efficiently in the company of people. Wolves are very awkward in a people environment. I see wolves and dogs as adapted to different niches, and so, in my brain, they qualify as different species. If the science world does insist on renaming the dog *Canis lupus familiaris*, there is one thing we must all remember. Just because dogs are renamed a subspecies of wolves does not make them wolves . . . To say that dogs have 100 percent the same genes as wolves does not mean we can treat them as if they were wolves."

Modern Breeds

Whether dogs are a subspecies of wolves or a separate species descended from wolves, everyone agrees that all breeds of domesticated dogs belong to a single species. The many dog breeds recognized around the world today differ widely in size, color, type of hair, and shape. Some breeds are relatively new, created within the past one hundred years or so. Even the oldest known variations are perhaps only 10,000 or 12,000 years old—a mere blink of an eye on the time scale of evolution. How did dogs get so varied in such a short time?

One clue lies in the biology of the genus *Canis*. Dogs, wolves, jackals, and coyotes all share the same genetic makeup. They have more chromosomes than any other mammal—seventy-eight in all (humans have forty-six). Mutations, or alterations in this genetic material, produce changes large and small in the structure and appearance of individual animals. Some mutations increase these animals' ability to survive—for example, by making them faster or stronger. Other mutations, such as deformities or coat markings that make it hard for the animals to blend into their surroundings, decrease survival ability. Still other mutations have no noticeable effect at all. In the wild, unfavorable mutations are generally weeded out quickly because the animals that have them do not thrive and breed. But if animals with variations do manage to survive and breed, either naturally or under the control of humans, those animals' characteristics will be passed to their offspring and on to later generations. Some research suggests that the inborn qualities related to what people call "tameness" in canids are genetically linked to physical features that are typically doglike, such as floppy ears, tails upturned at the end, and coats of varied colors. In other words, behavioral and physical traits may be tied together somehow and tend to be inherited together. If this proves to be true, it may explain how the ancestral wolves who came to live among humans—either selected by humans for tameness or because their naturally tame qualities led them to live near people— became doglike and variable in appearance.

Once early dog forms had begun to emerge, people emphasized the differences among types of dogs through artificial selection. By allowing only chosen pairs to mate, they strengthened the features or qualities they desired. This produced a number of very different types of dogs, most often bred to make them more useful for specific purposes such as hunting or herding. In modern times, dog breeding has become an art, and breeders have created entirely new varieties by blending existing breeds.

The dogs of the world can be grouped into broad, general categories by their appearance or by how people use them. For example, the American Kennel Club (AKC) has seven main categories for its dog shows. Sporting dogs, such as retrievers and spaniels, were originally bred to help hunters locate small game such as birds or to fetch the bodies of birds shot by hunters. Hounds, such as beagles and whippets, were developed to track large game. Some hounds rely on scent, others on sight. Working dogs, such as huskies and Saint Bernards, were bred for tasks such as pulling loads and rescuing people. Terriers were developed to dig in search of prey such as rodents and badgers. Herding dogs, such as the collie and the German shepherd, were bred to control livestock and protect it from predators. Toy dogs are small breeds developed as pets. Nonsporting dogs are large dogs that may once have been working dogs but are now chiefly pets such as poodles and bulldogs.

Within these groups are breeds, which are defined quite precisely. The AKC and other dog-fanciers' organizations worldwide recognize as many as four hundred breeds. Each breed is defined by a breed standard, a set of specific physical characteristics, such as size, head shape, length and color of hair, and so on. A dog must meet these standards to be registered as a member of its breed. A purebred is a dog whose ancestors have all

Various organizations classify dog breeds in different ways. One widely used system is that of the American Kennel Club, which divides breeds into seven main categories:

Sporting dogs, such as the Brittany spaniel

Hounds, such as the beagle

Herding dogs, such as the Australian shepherd

Nonsporting dogs, such as
the English bulldog

Toy dogs, such as
the shih tzu

Working dogs, such as
the Saint Bernard

Terriers, such as
the Jack Russell

come from the same breed, ever since that breed was officially recognized. It has a pedigree, which is a list of its ancestors that proves its purebred status.

Dogs whose parents did not belong to the same breed are called mixed-breed dogs, mutts, mongrels, or hybrids. They probably outnumber the purebred dogs of the world. Although mutts lack the glamour of a pedigree, they are often healthier

Mixed-breed dogs, sometimes called mongrels or mutts, may look like purebred dogs, but often they combine the characteristics of several breeds.

than some purebreds. Many breeds have been weakened by the inbreeding of closely related dogs or by breeders' emphasis on extreme, exaggerated physical features. Large breeds, for example, often suffer from an inherited weakness of the hip joints, and breeds with severely flattened noses, such as pugs and Pekingese, are prone to breathing problems. Many people find the mongrel, whose ancestry mixes traits from many kinds of dogs, a more "natural" kind of animal than a purebred whose breed would never have evolved in the wild.

3 The Biology of the Dog

It's a sunny summer afternoon in a city park. Couples hold hands on benches, watching skateboarders swoop and glide along paths. Nearby, kids run and play on a grassy lawn. One of them tosses a red plastic disk—or Frisbee—into the air, and it whirls over the grass. There is a sudden explosion of movement as a large, shaggy animal hurtles into view, charging after the Frisbee. It races down the field, its clawed paws digging into the lawn with each bounding step. The animal looks up, measures the height and speed of the Frisbee, and then, with a mighty push from its strongly muscled rear legs, leaps into the air. Its body turns and twists in midair and then—*snap!*—its powerful jaws snatch the moving disk out of the air. Then it trots proudly back to its young owner, tail wagging, ready for another chase.

A DOG PLAYING IN A PARK USES MUSCLES, SENSES, AND INSTINCTS THAT EVOLVED OVER MILLIONS OF YEARS TO MEET THE NEEDS OF A HUNTING ANIMAL.

The dog's game of catch in the park calls upon the same physical abilities that dogs' ancestors once used to catch their prey in the wild. Although humans have shaped the outer appearances of dogs, the dog's structure and senses are still much like those of its wild canine relatives, the wolf, jackal, and coyote.

The Body of the Dog

Dogs have no standard size. They range from tiny Chihuahuas, about 6 pounds (2.7 kg) in weight and 5 inches (13 cm) tall at the shoulder, to towering Great Danes, which are 39 inches (99 cm) tall, and sturdy mastiffs weighing 200 pounds (90 kg). Although all dogs are genetically able to interbreed, differences in size or leg length make it impossible for some pairs to mate.

Whatever its size, the dog's body is supported by its skeleton. A dog's skeleton has approximately 320 bones. (The number varies slightly because some dogs have more bones in their tails than others and also because male dogs have an additional bone, called the penile bone, in their sexual organ.) One of the main skeletal structures is the spine, which consists of small individual bones called vertebrae. The spine runs the length of the animal's body, from the base of the skull to the tip of the tail. It ends with a series of ever smaller bones called the caudal vertebrae, which make up the tail. The spine protects the spinal cord, which is the center of the animal's nervous system. Attached to the spine are the ribs, which form a cage that protects the dog's heart, lungs, liver, and stomach.

Also attached to the spine are two sets of bones called girdles. The shoulder girdle connects the dog's forelegs to the spine; the dog's hind legs are attached to the pelvic girdle. Dogs have elbows and knees. The elbows are on the forelegs—they are the backward-pointing joints where the leg bends when

Dog Skeleton

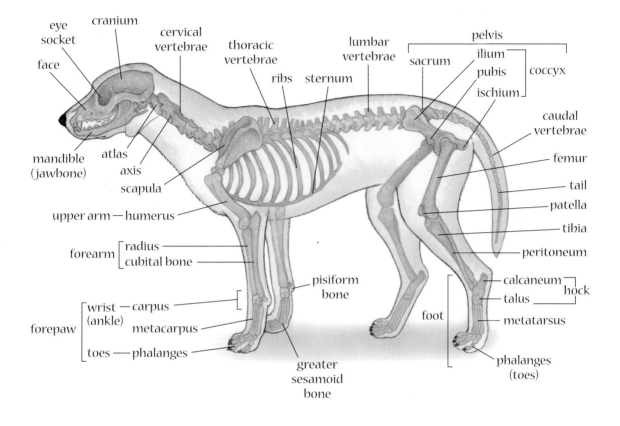

the dog takes a step or lifts a paw. The knees are the forward-pointing joints in the upper part of the hind legs. Further down the hind legs are joints that jut up and backward. The backward-pointing part of this joint is called the calcaneum. On a human foot, this bone is the heel.

Dogs have five toes on their front feet. The dog's hind feet generally have four toes each, although some dogs are born with shorter fifth claws, called dewclaws, on the hind feet (dewclaws usually do not reach the ground). The toes are cushioned with thick, springy mats of tough tissue called pads, and each toe

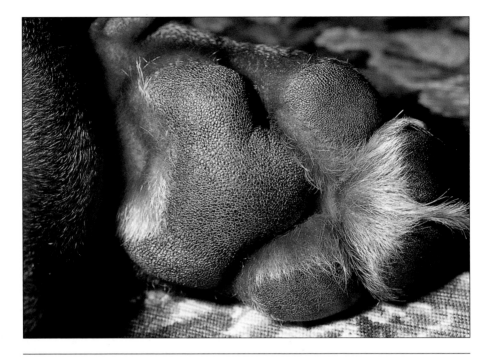

PADS OF THICK TISSUE CUSHION DOGS' TOES. THESE PADS ARE TOUGH, BUT ROUGH TERRAIN OR BROKEN GLASS CAN SCRATCH OR CUT THEM. INJURED PADS MAY BECOME INFECTED, WHICH IS WHY IT IS IMPORTANT TO CHECK DOGS' FEET FOR INJURIES AND TO KEEP THE PADS CLEAN.

is tipped with a claw. Unlike cats, dogs cannot draw their claws into their bodies when they are not using them. Some veterinarians and pet owners trim the claws of domestic dogs.

The skull of the dog protects the brain and the sense organs. It also houses the dog's teeth. These are vital tools for an animal that eats meat, whether it hunts live game or scavenges carcasses and garbage. Adult dogs normally have forty-two teeth. The dog uses its twelve small front teeth, called incisors, for gripping small things and nipping at burrs and fleas in its fur. The four long pointed teeth, one at each corner of the front of the mouth, are the canines, useful for piercing and holding. Behind them are sixteen premolars, including the carnassial teeth, and ten molars. These teeth cut, crush, chew, and grind. Skull shape is one of the highly variable features of dogs. Some dogs, such as collies and greyhounds, are short and broad, with a pronounced

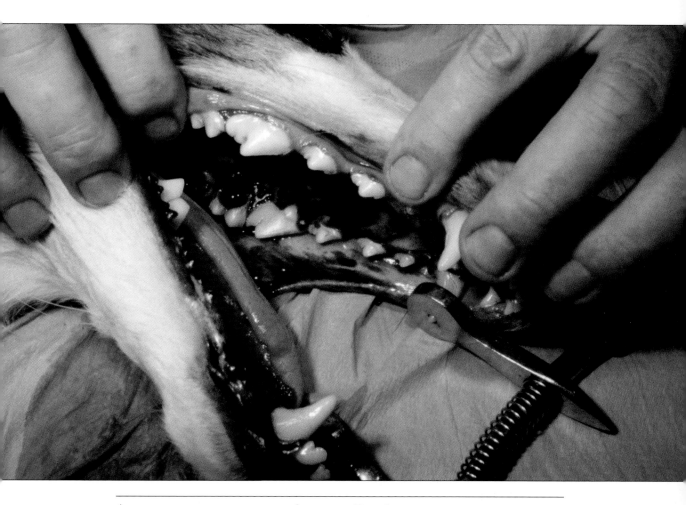

A VETERINARIAN EXAMINES A DOG'S MOUTH. DOGS' TEETH ARE LARGER THAN THOSE OF CATS BUT LESS SHARP.

marked stop, or angle, between the forehead and muzzle.

A dog's internal systems and organs are much like those of other canids and of mammals in general. The nervous system, which controls both movement and automatic processes such as breathing, consists of the brain and nerves. The respiratory system supplies the blood with oxygen from the air. Its chief organs are the two lungs, which are large relative to the animal's overall body size. These lungs can provide canids with enough oxygen for long periods of running. (Cats, in contrast, can run fast but tire quickly because their lungs are smaller in relation to their bodies.) The circulatory system, consisting of heart and blood vessels, moves blood through their body, carrying

Dog Organs

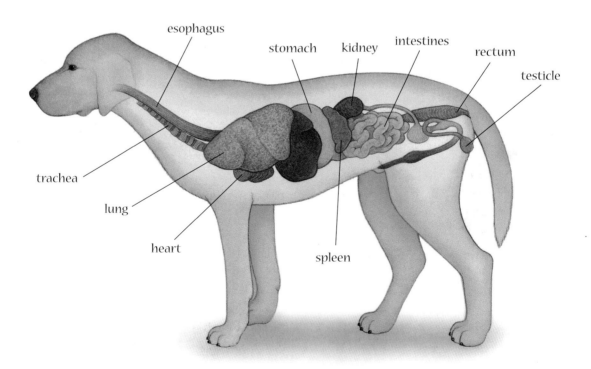

esophagus

stomach   kidney   intestines   rectum

testicle

trachea

lung

heart   spleen

oxygen and removing waste in the form of carbon dioxide. The digestive system—mouth, throat, stomach, liver, and intestines—takes in food and turns it into energy, eliminating solid waste in the form of feces from the anus at the end of the digestive tract. The urinary system, consisting of kidneys, bladder, and urethra, eliminates liquid waste as urine. The reproductive system consists of the sexual organs: testicles and penis in male dogs and ovaries and uterus in females. Females also have eight or ten mammary glands on the underside of their bodies. These produce milk for feeding the young.

The muscles around a dog's skeleton and organs allow the dog to move and give it strength. The dog's skin is attached to a

Dog Muscles

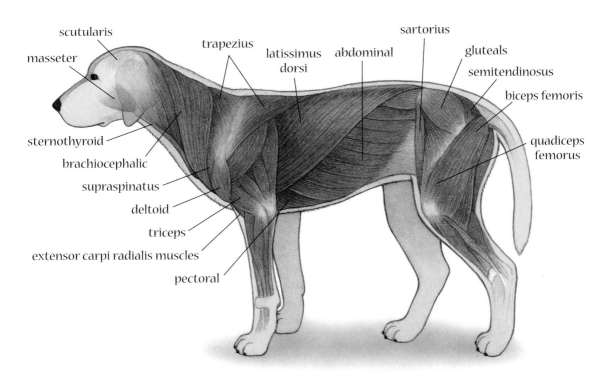

network of many small but strong muscles. These muscles let the skin move independently, as when a dog shakes itself dry or contracts the skin of its neck to make its hair bristle.

A dog's fur is made up of two types of hair. Fine hairs form an undercoat that provides warmth. The undercoat is denser on dogs that live in cold climates than on those that live in warm places. If hairs from the undercoat are shed in the spring, the undercoat regains its thickness in the fall. Longer, thicker hairs called guard hairs form the top coat. Oils in the guard hairs make the dog's coat shiny and provide some protection from water. The overall appearance of a dog's fur is created by the texture, color, and markings of the top coat. Dogs' coats come in many

Dog Body

textures: long and silky, bushy and thick, wiry and tightly curled, and short and smooth. Colors and markings are also quite variable. Some breeds have coats that are more than one color, and even within a single litter individual pups may be born with different colors and markings.

Canine Senses

A third type of hair grows on the dog's face. These hairs, called tactile hairs, are found around the eyes and nose and on the cheeks. The longest, thickest tactile hairs are grouped at the front of the muzzle and are sometimes called whiskers. No one is certain of the purpose of the tactile hairs, but they may help dogs "feel" their way in tight places or in darkness. A dog's paws and its long, flexible tongue are also organs of touch that the animal uses to explore its environment.

Dogs see the world differently than humans do. Most experts believe that dogs do not see colors. Some think that dogs see only shades of gray, while others believe that dogs interpret all colors as shades of red. A dog's field of vision is wider than a human's because a dog's eyes are placed farther apart and toward the sides of its head. This means that dogs are better at seeing things off to either side than people are. In general, though, canine eyesight is not as good as human sight, especially close up. Dogs are much better at noticing movement than they are at recognizing shapes. The best vision occurs among borzois and other hounds that have been bred over the centuries to hunt by sight. All dogs and other canids have a shiny membrane called the *tapetum lucidum* at the back of each eye. The membrane improves their night vision by gathering and reflecting available light. It also makes their eyes seem to glow when a light falls upon them at night.

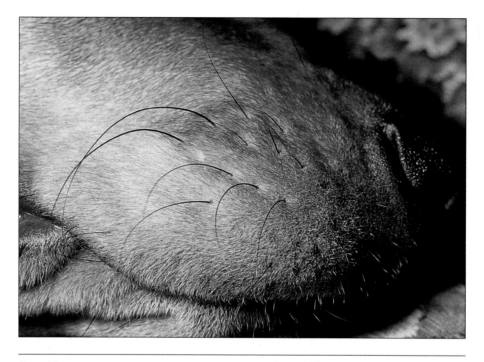

A DOG'S WHISKERS ARE PART OF ITS SENSE OF TOUCH. WHEN A DOG SHEDS OR LOSES A WHISKER, A NEW ONE GROWS TO TAKE ITS PLACE.

For information about the world around them, dogs rely more on hearing than on sight. All wild canids have upright triangular ears that can move independently to help the animals pinpoint the location of sounds. Some domestic dogs also have erect ears, but many have ears that flop forward. Floppy ears is a mutation that does not survive in wolf populations. Humans, however, have bred long ears into some kinds of dogs, such as spaniels and beagles. Dogs with erect ears have slightly keener hearing than those with floppy ears. This is an advantage in hunting for prey and avoiding predators—but these things are not part of most domestic dogs' lives. Some people have their

WHEN A DOG'S EARS ARE ERECT, YOU KNOW IT IS LISTENING TO SOMETHING—BUT IN MODERN LIFE, IT IS MORE LIKELY TO BE A CAN OPENER THAN A PREDATOR.

dogs' long ears cropped, or cut, to produce a more alert and watchful appearance. This is especially true with breeds such as the Doberman pinschers. In some countries and states, cropping has been outlawed as unnecessarily cruel, along with docking, the surgical shortening of a dog's tail to produce a stump for reasons of appearance only.

No matter how its ears are shaped, a dog can hear much better than a human. Not only can a dog pinpoint the location and direction of sounds, but it can also hear faint, distant sounds. Dogs are especially good at hearing high-pitched noises, even ones that humans cannot hear in what is called the ultrasonic range. Some dog owners and trainers use ultrasonic whistles— a dog can hear the whistle, but there is no piercing blast to annoy the neighbors.

Dogs learn most about their world through scent, their most highly developed sense. The keenness of their sense of smell is due to the olfactory mucus membrane, a moist and sensitive tissue inside the nose. A typical human's olfactory membrane covers less than a square inch (about 5 cm²) and has about half a million cells that serve as scent receptors. But the membrane of a dog would cover more than 18 square inches (120 cm²) if spread out flat. It has an average of about 200 million receptor cells. A dog that wants to sniff something or to follow a scent may lick its nose—the saliva helps the outer part of the nose trap scent molecules from the air.

In one test of dogs' sense of smell, experimenters mixed a single drop of vinegar into 220 gallons (1,000 l) of water, and then mixed a single drop of that mixture into another 220 gallons of water. Dogs could still detect the scent of vinegar in the final mixture. Dogs are even better at detecting the odors of fatty acids, such as those contained in animal tissue. Their exceptional ability to identify these acids allows them to track game, locate

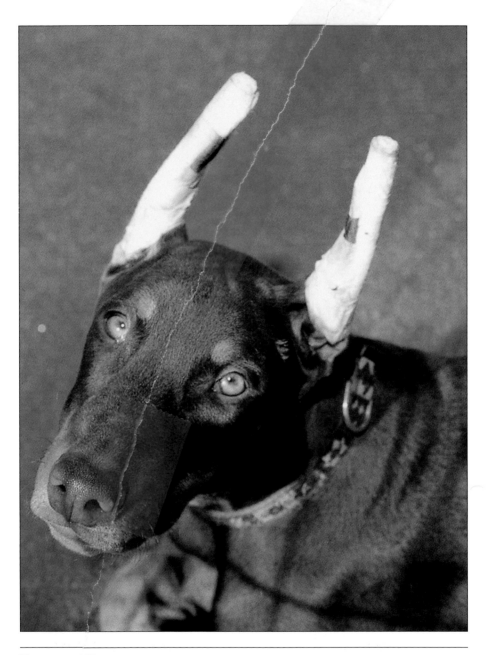

This young Doberman Pinscher has had its ears surgically shortened to make them stand up erect when the bandages are removed. Some dog owners feel that this operation, now banned as unnecessary and cruel in some countries, gives their animals a more alert appearance.

LIKE ALL DOGS, THIS GOLDEN RETRIEVER RELIES ON ITS NOSE FOR A GREAT DEAL OF
INFORMATION ABOUT THE WORLD AROUND IT. A DOG'S MOST HIGHLY DEVELOPED
SENSE IS SCENT, USED FOR COMMUNICATION AS WELL AS HUNTING.

mates, and recognize each other and other familiar animals, including humans. Some breeds have such a well developed sense of smell that they can follow a person's trail after smelling a piece of that person's clothing.

Where health problems are concerned, some dogs have a huge advantage over other canids. They belong to owners who take them to veterinarians. Veterinary care can protect dogs against some diseases and correct many health problems. But whether they receive veterinary care or not, all dogs face a number of common health problems.

Some problems are dental. Broken teeth or diseased gums can interfere with eating. Without care, a dog suffering severe dental problems can starve to death. Dogs can also fall victim to contagious diseases. Leptospirosis attacks the kidneys. Caused by bacteria, it travels from dog to dog through the urine of infected animals. Canine parvovirus can kill a dog in as little as twenty-four hours through severe diarrhea and dehydration. The viral disease called distemper usually attacks young dogs and can strike at the digestive, respiratory, or nervous system. Vaccinations are available to protect dogs from these diseases.

A vaccination against rabies also exists. Rabies, a viral disease that destroys the nervous system, can affect any mammal bitten by a rabid, or infected, host. Rabies affects dogs in two ways. The raging stage of rabies makes dogs violently excited, so that they attack and bite everything around them. The paralytic stage locks a dog's jaws shut so that it cannot drink, eat, or swallow saliva (which flows or foams out through the locked jaws). There is no cure for rabies—once the disease sets in, the animal must be destroyed.

Parasites are organisms that live on or in other organisms. A parasite provides no benefit to the host animal—in fact, its presence or activities may be dangerous, or at least uncomfortable. Dogs are plagued by many kinds of parasites. Fleas, ticks, and mange (skin or ear irritation cause by microscopic parasites)

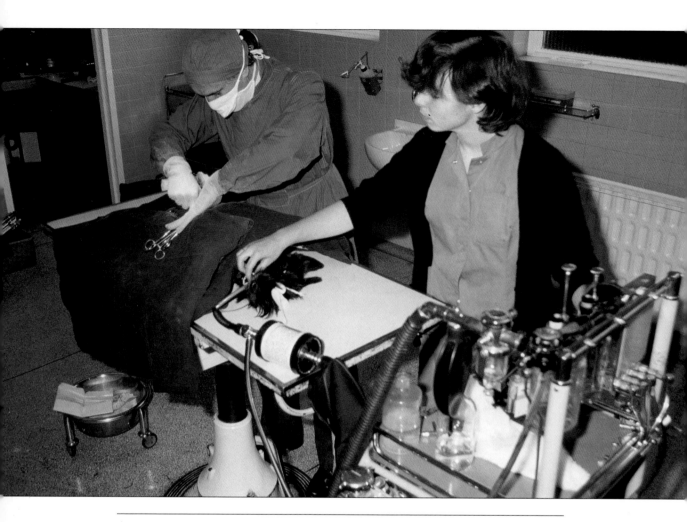

A VETERINARY SURGEON OPERATES ON A DOG. DOGS LUCKY ENOUGH TO RECEIVE
HIGH-QUALITY AND COSTLY VETERINARY CARE MAY NOW BE TREATED FOR CANCER,
KIDNEY DISEASE, AND OTHER ONCE-FATAL CONDITIONS.

affect a dog on the outside, but some parasites inside a dog can
be more destructive. These include tapeworms, roundworms,
and whipworms, all of which can infect dogs that eat food,
carcasses, or feces that contain the worms or their eggs. Heart-
worms are carried by mosquitoes and are most common in

warm climates. They grow and multiply inside a dog's heart and can destroy its major organs. Hookworms are tiny parasites that dogs can pick up by eating off the ground. Multiplying quickly, they cause weakness, weight loss, and diarrhea, and they can be fatal to young dogs. A mother dog who is infested with hookworms may pass these parasites to her puppies in the uterus or in her milk. Veterinarians can treat these parasitic infestations.

Many dogs recover from some health problems, or at least manage to endure them, without treatment. There is no doubt, however, that regular basic care, such as teeth cleanings, vaccinations, and wormings, improves the quality and length of life for those dogs lucky enough to receive it.

4 Canine Behavior

"Let dogs delight to bark and bite," says a line from a song written in England in 1715, making the point that it is a dog's nature to bark and to bite. Sometimes "the bark is worse than the bite," as another old saying goes, meaning that a dog who raises a great fuss may be harmless in the end. Barking, biting, and other kinds of behavior are how a dog relates to its surroundings, including the people around it. But a dog doesn't have to rely on a bite to get its message across—dogs can be very communicative to those who understand their body language and the sounds they make.

Pack Life

Dogs can learn to do many things they would not normally do in the wild, and often they readily adopt forms of behavior that please the people with whom they live. Many dogs can do tricks,

A BORDER COLLIE IN THE POSITION CALLED PLAY-BOWING.
DOGS TAKE THIS POSITION TOWARD THEIR OWNERS OR
OTHER PEOPLE WHEN THEY WANT TO BE PETTED OR TO PLAY.

for example, and most domestic dogs are housebroken, which means that they have learned not to empty their bladders and bowels inside houses. But much of a dog's behavior is not learned. It is instinctive, driven by an inborn compulsion to do certain things in a certain way. No owner teaches a pet dog to roll in strong-smelling substances such as garbage, rotting carcasses, or animal feces. Dogs just do so instinctively, if given the chance, because many wild predators do so—perhaps to hide their own scent.

The key to understanding dog behavior is to remember that dogs originated from wolves. Wolves are social animals that live in packs, which usually consist of a mating pair and their growing offspring. Pack life has definite social organizations and rules of behavior. Much of what dogs do, especially when relating to other dogs or to their human owners or families, can be understood in terms of pack behavior. For example, each pack has a leader, or dominant animal. The others are submissive, which means that they accept the leader's domination. Because size and strength help determine who becomes a leader, pack leaders are usually male. Although a pack may contain half a dozen males old enough to breed, the leader is the only one who mates. Another wolf can obtain breeding rights in one of two ways—either by finding a mate and moving to a new territory, or, less often, by successfully challenging the leader, defeating him or driving him off and taking his place.

Few domestic dogs today live in packs. For most, pack experience is limited to a few weeks or months with their littermates after they are born. But whenever two or three dogs live together or are in close contact, one of them, male or female, eventually emerges as the leader. The dominant dog may eat first, occupy a favored sleeping place, shove the other dogs aside to greet the owner, take toys away from the others

Wolves live in packs. Dogs, their close relatives, are also adapted to live in close contact with others. For most domestic dogs, the "pack" is their human family.

whenever it wants, or demonstrate its dominance in other ways.

A dog's human family also becomes something like a pack. Some dog-behavior experts and dog trainers claim that a dog must be trained to regard its primary owner as its pack leader, and that if the dog is not properly trained when young, it will attempt to dominate its owner. Other experts believe that it is not necessarily true that dogs regard people in the same way that they view other dogs. But it is true that dogs are adapted to be social rather than solitary and that dogs who are left alone for long periods of time show signs of unhappiness and distress. They may be nervous, depressed, listless, or snappish. They may gain or lose weight. Dogs are happiest when they are doing what comes naturally, which means relating to other familiar beings on a daily basis. Wolves within a pack express their connection through comforting, reassuring physical contact, such as sniffing and rubbing their faces against each other, gentle nipping, playing and romping together, or resting and sleeping side by side. Often a wolf will rest its head on a pack mate's back. Dogs have the same urges, which is why they enjoy being petted or brushed, sleeping on their owners' beds, having their bellies rubbed, and resting their heads on their owners' knees or in their laps.

Another aspect of pack behavior is protecting the pack's territory and its young. Male wolves mark their territory by scratching up mounds of dirt and by depositing urine, feces, and scent from a gland near the anus. Females also mark, but less

A GOLDEN RETRIEVER CHECKS A FIRE HYDRANT FOR THE SCENT MARKINGS OF OTHER DOGS. THESE MARKINGS TELL THE RETRIEVER WHAT OTHER DOGS HAVE PASSED THAT SPOT AND HOW LONG AGO.

often. These markings help animals find their way around their own territory and warn other animals to stay away. Dogs also mark their territory, although they can be trained not to do so indoors. Part of a dog's ritual when taken for a walk is to refresh its own scent markings and to check other dogs' markings to see who has been around. The instinct to protect home territory and other pack members becomes a useful trait in a guard dog or watchdog. Training can strengthen that instinct.

In addition to being social and territorial animals, dogs are also predators. Dogs today do not hunt for food—they are fed by their owners or they scavenge scraps and waste. Still, many dogs chase moving objects in the same way that their wild ancestors chased deer and other prey. This is why dogs like to chase thrown balls or sticks. With a little encouragement they learn to bring the objects back to their owners for another throw. Sometimes the chase instinct leads dogs into trouble. Chasing cars is one example, and dogs who are allowed to roam outside without leashes must be trained not to do so. A dog's inherited behavior patterns do not prepare it to survive in traffic.

Everyday Activities

Social animals must be able to communicate with one another, and dogs are no exception. They communicate with both sound and body language. Barking is the most commonly produced noise. Wolves bark rarely, but because people valued watchdogs that barked, the trait of barking became stronger as people selected and bred dogs over the years. A bark can be a friendly greeting, an alarm, a warning, or simply the dog's way of saying, "I am here." Barking ranges from the full-throated woofing of a large, deep-chested dog to the more shrill yipping of a toy dog. A growl or a snarl is a warning that the dog is feeling anxious or

MANY DOG OWNERS HAVE A FEW WELL-CHEWED TENNIS BALLS AROUND THEIR
HOUSES. DOGS LOVE CHASING AND CATCHING THESE BALLS, AND DOGS THAT ARE
GOOD SWIMMERS WILL JOYOUSLY JUMP INTO LAKES OR STREAMS IN PURSUIT OF A
THROWN BALL.

aggressive. Some dogs also howl, and many owners report that sirens, bells, or certain kinds of music seem to inspire dogs to howl as though they were singing along. Puppies whimper when they are separated from their mothers, and an older dog may whimper in times of distress or yelp if it is surprised or hurt. Dogs not only make sounds but are sensitive to sounds made by those around them. Domestic dogs soon learn to interpret the significance of their owners' tone of voice, such as the difference between "*Good* boy!" and "No! Bad dog!"

Dogs' body language is very expressive. Ears, tail, and overall posture can speak volumes about an animal's emotions and intentions. Ears raised or cocked forward mean that a dog is interested, attentive, or curious. Relaxed ears show that the dog is at ease. Ears flattened back against the side of the dog's head can be a sign of meekness and submission to a more dominant individual, but they also can be a threatening sign, a warning that the dog is angry and may be provoked to fight. Flattened ears together with eyes lowered or turned away equals submission; when paired with a direct stare, the behavior is threatening. Other signs of submission include tucking the tail between the legs, pulling the lips back into an expression that resembles a smile, closing the jaws, lowering the head, crouching, and lying on one side or even on the back to expose the defenseless stomach. All of these signals say, "I'm not going to do anything to

THE BARED TEETH OF THIS GUARD DOG ARE A SIGN THAT THIS IS NOT A FRIENDLY, WELCOMING BARK. DOGS BARK AS WARNINGS AND ALSO TO EXPRESS CURIOSITY, EXCITEMENT, AND PLEASURE. THE BODY LANGUAGE THAT ACCOMPANIES EACH BARK MAKES THE DOG'S MEANING CLEAR.

POSTURE REVEALS THE RELATIONSHIP BETWEEN THESE TWO DOGS. THE GOLDEN RETRIEVER IS IN A SUBMISSIVE POSITION, AND THE BLACK NEWFOUNDLAND IS THE DOMINANT ANIMAL.

you—don't hurt me." Such behavior does not necessarily mean that the dog is afraid. Submissive postures can also be a sign that the dog feels relaxed and comfortable. A wagging tail and wriggling body are greetings and signs of happiness. In contrast, a dog that opens its jaws, shows its teeth, raises and stiffens its tail, and bristles up the hair on its neck and back is saying, "I'm in charge here—don't come a step closer."

Dogs belong to the order of Carnivora, but they eat more than just meat. Wolves consume some grains, fruits, and vegetables, usually by eating the stomachs of their prey, although sometimes they chew on grass or eat fallen fruit. Dogs too require some grains and vegetables in their diet for proper nutrition. Commercially prepared dog foods, both canned and dry, usually contain the right mix of ingredients in the form of rice or wheat, carrots, and corn or sunflower oil along with chopped or ground meat. It is a mistake, however, to feed a dog a true vegetarian diet. People can live without eating meat so long as they are careful to consume the proper blend of nutrients, but dogs are adapted to eat animal protein and must do so to be as healthy as possible. It is also a good idea to give dogs hard, dry biscuits to chew from time to time, as this cleans their teeth.

The eating habits of dogs reflect their wild pack ancestry. Pack animals generally compete for food and eat quickly—this is the origin of the phrase "wolfing your food." As a result, dogs also tend to eat rapidly. Because wild animals adapted to eating as much food as possible whenever they made a kill, dogs will generally overeat if they are given unlimited access to food.

Dogs can sleep either by day or by night. Those who live with people generally get used to sleeping when their owners sleep, although they need more sleep than humans and will nap frequently during their owners' waking hours. Dogs that live on their own tend to sleep whenever they are full and wherever they feel safest. Wild canids like to sleep in dens, hollows or secluded spots where they feel comfortable and secure. Dogs are no different. A dog likes to have a sleeping place it can call its own, whether it is a blanket, a crate, a particular chair, or the foot of its owner's bed.

All dogs devote a certain amount of their waking time to grooming themselves. The most common way of doing this is by

DOGS SLEEP MORE THAN PEOPLE DO. MANY DOMESTIC DOGS NOT ONLY SLEEP THROUGH THE NIGHT BUT ALSO, LIKE THIS GREAT DANE COMFORTABLY SPRAWLED ACROSS ITS OWNER'S COUCH, NAP DURING THE DAY AS WELL.

shaking, which removes water and dirt from the coat. A dog may also clean its coat by rolling in sand or on grass. It scratches its body with the claws of its hind feet to spread natural oils from skin glands through its fur, and it scratches its ears to remove fleas, ticks, or wax. Dogs also use their mouths in grooming. They nip at fleas, burrs, or snarls in their fur, and they lick their anal regions to keep them clean. Dogs also lick wounds such as scratches or cuts—some experts believe that chemicals in their saliva help clean these injuries and prevent infection.

Intelligence

Are dogs intelligent? Most dog owners would answer, "Yes, absolutely," and then tell you how clever their own dogs are. Popular literature and urban legend are full of stories about dogs who save their owners' lives, make their way home over great distances, or simply seem to "know" that their owner is on the way home from work well before he or she arrives. Most such stories are poorly documented, and even when they can be proved, the dogs' feats can generally be explained by instinct or training. They do not mean that dogs are intelligent in the way that people are.

Intelligence is difficult to measure in human beings, and even experts disagree about how to define it. The task is no easier in dogs. Scientists and dog trainers know, however, that dogs do not appear to have the powers of creative thought or problem solving. They *are* good at remembering connections between things. With very little experience a dog can learn to connect seeing its leash with going for a walk or hearing the cupboard door open with getting a treat. From these associations it is a short step to carrying the leash in its mouth when it wants to go out or pawing the cupboard door when it wants a treat.

Most dogs are sensitive to their owners' moods and eager to please. In addition, they like to play. They often seem to enjoy being trained, regarding training as a kind of game. They learn best when rewarded for performing well with a treat or a sign of affection. Dogs can be trained to remember and obey as many as fifty spoken commands. They can also respond to unspoken

A GUIDE DOG HELPS ITS BLIND OWNER NAVIGATE CITY SIDEWALKS. DOGS HAVE GOOD
MEMORIES, AND THEY ALSO HAVE THE DESIRE TO FORM CLOSE BONDS WITH THEIR
OWNERS. THIS COMBINATION OF TRAITS MAKES THEM EXCELLENT HELPERS WHEN
PROPERLY TRAINED.

commands, such as hand gestures and even facial expressions. The combination of eagerness to please, their ability to associate things and events, and their natural communicativeness means that dogs can be trained to perform a number of complex tasks, from riding on horseback in a circus to guiding a blind person along a busy city street.

5 The Life Cycle

Anyone who has ever taken a puppy for a walk knows that puppies are surefire crowd pleasers. Grins appear on strangers' faces. Children "ooh" and "aah" and instinctively try to pet these lively, soft creatures. Puppies are so endearing that they have become a symbol of happiness and cuteness. According to one view of dog origins, dogs owe their very existence to this cuteness. This view holds that wolf pups, with their big heads and eyes, plump bodies, uncoordinated movements, and helpless whimpering, reminded early humans of their own infants. The same instinct that drives people to care for their own young led them to adopt and care for pups, and so the process of turning wolves into dogs began. Some biologists have even suggested that breeding by humans has created dogs—at

A LABRADOR RETRIEVER WITH HER PUPPIES.

least in some breeds—that keep features of puppyhood, such as rounded heads and playfulness, throughout their lives.

Courtship and Mating

A dog's life begins with the mating of its parents. Whether the partners choose themselves or are put together by breeders, their mating follows a set pattern. Male dogs can mate at any time, but bitches, as female dogs are called, mate only when they are in a condition called estrus (a dog in estrus is sometimes said to be in season or in heat). Bitches come into estrus twice a year, and each estrus lasts for two to three weeks. During this time their bodies give off hormones, chemical signals that male dogs can smell in the females' urine and scent markings. These chemicals attract males, who may fight for the chance to mate with a female. Female dogs, however, have the final say in choosing partners, and they may reject males who are too aggressive. During estrus, a female may mate with several different males. Dogs do not usually form permanent pair bonds or mating couples unless they belong to the same household.

Before mating, the two dogs engage in a courtship ritual. The male dog approaches the female, showing his interest with a raised tail. If the female is not at all interested, she may snap at him to drive him away or run away herself. But if she is feeling ready to mate, she will respond with signs of playfulness, such as jumping, "bowing" by lowering the front part of her body, wagging her tail, and perhaps playfully nipping the male or jumping on his back. The two dogs then begin mock-wrestling, sometimes giving low growls. During this contact, the female becomes familiar with the scent of the male and comfortable with his close presence. They break from play to sniff each other, especially around the scent glands and sexual organs. When the female is ready to mate, she stands still, holding her tail to one side. The male approaches cautiously—at this stage she could still change her mind and snap at him. If she allows him to stand next to her, he then moves behind her and rises onto his hind legs, clasping her around the middle with his forelegs. The dogs mate in this position.

The sexual act takes only moments, but after it is completed, the male's still-swollen penis cannot immediately be withdrawn from the female's body. Biologists think that male dogs evolved this feature to prevent other males from mating immediately after with the females. The two animals generally remain linked together for fifteen minutes to half an hour. During this time the male is likely to change position so that he is facing away from the female. After the two animals have uncoupled, they may mate again within a few hours or days or go their separate ways.

After estrus, hormones in the female's body cause her to act pregnant, even if she is not. Pregnancy behavior includes making a den in which to give birth. An outdoor dog may dig a hole or find a den under a porch, while an indoor dog will probably choose a closet or a private space under a bed or chair. She may carry favorite toys or soft items such as socks into the den and muzzle them as though she were grooming pups. This behavior lasts for about two months. In cases where the female has not become pregnant, this period is called a false pregnancy. If the female *is* pregnant, her belly will begin to swell during the second month, and she will whelp, or give birth, about sixty-three days after mating. Some small dogs deliver fewer than four puppies, and sometimes only one. Bigger dogs produce litters of four to ten puppies. Larger litters sometimes occur, although they are likely to include some small and sickly pups that will not thrive. Occasionally mother dogs kill some of their pups if they sense that the young are sick or deformed in any way.

A PREGNANT DOG IS LIKELY TO SPEND A LOT OF TIME IN THE SAFE, COMFORTABLE NEST WHERE SHE PLANS TO DELIVER HER YOUNG.

Puppyhood

A mother's duties begin as soon as a puppy is born. She licks it clean at once, removing the birth sac so that the pup can breathe. Licking also warms the pup, stimulates it to empty its bladder and bowels for the first time, and creates a bond between mother and puppy by bathing the infant in its mother's scent. Knowing her scent will help the puppy return to her after squirming away. A newborn puppy is drawn by instinct to the warmth of its mother's belly and to the smell of milk from her mammary glands. She may nudge the puppy into position so that it can begin suckling.

Puppies are quite helpless for the first few weeks of their lives. They can roll over and push themselves around on their bellies, but they cannot walk. Their eyes and ears are closed. Scent, the

A Norfolk terrier nurses her litter of five-day-old puppies. Puppies' digestive systems develop quickly, and in less than three weeks these pups will be ready to sample solid food.

sense of touch, and the craving for warmth help them stay close to their mother and to one another. If they wander away, they squeak or whimper until she finds them. They spend a lot of time sleeping, and when they are not sleeping they are usually nursing from their mother. A mother dog is extremely protective of young puppies and may attack any person or animal who approaches them, although she will probably let members of her own human family look at them and handle them—under her close and anxious supervision. It is good for puppies who will become pets to be stroked or cuddled by people every day, so that they become used to the scents, voices, and touches of humans. This will make it easier for them to form connections with people later on in their lives.

A puppy's world begins to expand after about two weeks. Its eyes open when it is ten to fifteen days old, although the sense of sight does not fully develop for another few weeks. The puppy's ear canals open at around the same time, and it begins to take in the sounds of the world around it. Most pups begin walking when they are about two weeks old, although they remain unsteady or wobbly for another week or so. At three weeks of age they can wag their tails and bark. By five or six weeks they have begun to run and jump.

Once they have mastered the ability to move around, puppies tend to follow their mother wherever she goes. Since birth they have lived entirely on her milk. Now, at about three weeks of age, they are ready to begin eating solid food. Wild canids introduce their young to solid food by vomiting it up for them to eat. Some dogs do this also, but dogs who live with people are more likely to let their owners provide the food. Although a pup can live entirely on solid food by six weeks of age, many puppies try to keep nursing because of the comfort of the familiar mother-pup bond. Eventually the mother dog will refuse to let them nurse. At this point the young dogs are considered weaned.

Beyond eating and sleeping, a puppy has two main activities: exploring its environment and playing. Puppies are instinctively curious about the world, eager to sniff, touch, taste, and chew everything in it. This process of exploration not only teaches them about the world they inhabit but also sharpens their senses and their muscle coordination. Research has shown that puppies that are allowed to explore their surroundings and handle a variety of objects have greater brain development than those confined to small spaces with only a few toys or things to spark their curiosity. Yet puppies need to be kept safe—very young dogs feel no fear of people or other animals. They become more cautious when they are about two months old.

Play is a big part of a puppy's world. Its principal playmates are its littermates, although puppies will also play with older dogs, people, and even other animals such as cats and rabbits. In wild canids, play is practice for survival activities such as hunting and defending territory. For dogs, play builds strength and movement skills and teaches a young dog how to interact with others in a social setting. Through chasing, wrestling, and play fighting with gentle bites, the littermates establish an order of dominance. They also learn to work as a team and form bonds that last throughout their lives—dogs that have been separated from their siblings for years appear to recognize them at once. Reunited siblings sometimes play together like puppies.

The behavior patterns established during the second and third months of life determine to a large extent how shy or aggressive a dog will be and how well it will get along with others. Dog trainers agree that the best time to introduce a dog to the human family that will become its "pack" is when it is six to eight weeks old, although older dogs that have been well socialized can join a canine or human group at any age.

THIS FOUR-MONTH-OLD
LABRADOR RETRIEVER IS
DOING WHAT COMES NATU-
RALLY—LABS ARE GOOD
AT BOTH SWIMMING AND
FETCHING THINGS. ACTIVE
PLAY HELPS PUPPIES AND
YOUNG DOGS DEVELOP
STRENGTH AND SKILLS.

Adulthood

Dogs are considered whelps, or subadults, until they are a year old. The majority of dogs achieve their adult height before that time, but they gain weight and body mass into the second year of life. Play does not end when puppyhood is over, however. One reason people like dogs is that even adult dogs like to play, and one reason dogs like to play is that people have bred that characteristic into them. After puppyhood, though, a dog's play generally becomes calmer. The wild, unfocused energy of the younger days can be channeled into walks, structured games such as catch, and training.

Both male and female dogs may become sexually mature, or physically able to reproduce, before they are full-grown. Sexual behavior can be troublesome in a pet dog. Females in estrus attract male dogs and may act nervous or aggressive. Sexually active males spray urine and leave scent marks, and they too may act aggressive or competitive. For many owners the solution is to have the dogs' sexual organs (testicles in male dogs, ovaries in female ones) surgically removed by a veterinarian. This safe and widely used process is called neutering on a male and spaying on a female. Animal welfare groups encourage neutering and spaying to prevent the birth of unwanted puppies that may be neglected or mistreated. Such births add to the enormous number of unwanted dogs leading a forlorn life on the streets or being put to death in animal shelters and city pounds.

A dog's need for affection and social interaction does not disappear as it gets older, but older dogs can sometimes become short-tempered and snappish. This is especially true of dogs who begin to have difficulty seeing and hearing; they are easily startled by unexpected movements or sounds. Older dogs prefer

As dogs move from puppyhood into adulthood, the energy that once went into play can be channeled into training. This German shepherd is learning to obey commands while on a leash.

familiar surroundings and may be distressed by changes, even by something as simple as a rearrangement of the furniture.

Folk wisdom says that a year in a dog's life equals seven in a human life. This traditional saying is meaningless because dogs mature and age very differently than humans do. Dogs are dependent upon their mothers for a shorter percentage of their lives and they reach sexual maturity earlier. In addition, dogs' life spans are highly variable. With proper care and a healthy way of life, small and middle-sized dogs generally live for fifteen years or longer. Larger animals generally have life spans in the

LOOKING VERY MUCH LIKE THE ANCIENT EGYPTIAN DOG STATUE SHOWN IN CHAPTER 1, THIS MODERN MONUMENT RESTS ATOP A DOG'S GRAVE IN HIGHGATE CEMETERY, LONDON.

range of nine to twelve years, although there are plenty of exceptions. One modern dog is known to have reached twenty-nine years of age. Improvements in veterinary care and the development of special foods for older dogs may lead to more and more dogs living into their late teens.

People provide food and shelter for many dogs today. They determine how their dogs will live—and often, they also control when and how their dogs die. In cases of injury, incurable illness, or simply the breakdown of the body due to old age, many dog owners choose to give their animals an easy and painless death with an overdose of sleeping drugs administered by a veterinarian. Common causes of canine death include heart disease, kidney failure, traffic accidents, and, for scavengers, diseases caused by malnutrition. People who have cherished dogs in life sometimes treat the dogs' deaths as they would treat those of loved family members, with funerals or memorials. Special cemeteries exist so that dog owners can have the remains of their pets buried, just as the ancient Egyptians did thousands of years ago.

6 A World of Dogs

A silky Pomeranian winning prizes at a dog show and a scabby pariah scavenging for scraps at a village dump seem like very different animals, but they are biologically the same. They are the same in another way, too—both of them live in some sort of relation to human beings. Wild canids became dogs through their associations with humans, and today all dogs, from pampered pet to despised pest, live in a world defined by humans. Even dogs that do not have any direct contact with people often get at least some of their food from humans. This can be in the form of garbage, small or young livestock, or the rats and mice that are attracted to human dwellings and places where people store grain.

Although no one knows exactly how many dogs live in the world today, biologist Raymond Coppinger has estimated the

THE POMERANIAN IS ONE OF THE BREEDS CALLED TOY DOGS, DEVELOPED TO BE HOUSEHOLD PETS. MOST POMERANIANS ARE EXPENSIVE AND TREASURED COMPANIONS. MANY OF THE WORLD'S DOGS, HOWEVER, LEAD VERY DIFFERENT LIVES.

worldwide dog population at 400 million. This figure includes dogs living in a wide range of circumstances. The dog that is most familiar to people in North America, Great Britain, and western Europe is the household pet. But the modern Western way of regarding dogs as pets, almost as family members, has not been typical throughout history, and it is not universal in the world today.

Dogs have met harsh treatment in many times and places. In medieval Europe they were used in baiting, a form of entertainment that pitted dogs against wild animals such as bears or boars. Today some cultures enjoy dogfights in which two dogs, perhaps specially trained to fight or starved and mistreated to make them hostile, battle each other, sometimes to death, in front of spectators. Someone from Great Britain or Virginia might be shocked by this practice but still take part in the traditional British sport of foxhunting, in which dogs chase and kill their relatives, foxes.

Modern laws against cruelty to animals have ended many forms of dog abuse, or at least made them illegal and driven them underground. Other uses of dogs continue to spark debate. For example, dogs are used to take the place of people in scientific experiments. In 1957, Russia (then a part of the Soviet Union) made a hero out of Laika, the first dog sent into space, although the dog suffered a lingering and painful death in her capsule. Other dogs are used to test drugs and surgical procedures. Some animal-rights activists want to see all such practices stopped, no matter what animals are involved. Many people, however, can accept rats or mice as experimental subjects but are upset by the thought of dogs in the same circumstances.

The eating of dogs arouses similar feelings. Dogs have traditionally been used as food in many parts of eastern and southeastern Asia, and Asian people in many parts of the world still

IN VIETNAM, A VENDOR SELLS DOGS FROM THE BACK OF HIS BICYCLE. THESE DOGS
WILL BE EATEN, A COMMON PRACTICE IN MANY COUNTRIES.

eat dog meat. In 2002, with the announcement that the World
Cup soccer match was to be held in South Korea, where dog
meat is sold and consumed, activists from around the world
called upon the Korean people to abandon the practice. French
actress-turned-activist Brigitte Bardot declared, "I accept that

many people eat beef, but a cultured country does not allow its people to eat dogs." In response, American columnist William Saletan questioned whether dogs should be regarded as different from other animals simply because some cultures make pets and friends of them (until recent times Koreans did not keep dogs as pets). He argued that if it is wrong to eat dog, then it is equally wrong to eat pig and cow, but if it is all right to eat pig and cow, then it is also all right to eat dog. The question is likely to remain under discussion not just in Asia but also in the United States, where the sale of dog meat is legal in forty-four states.

While there have always been people who love dogs, not every culture or every individual has considered the dog to be "man's best friend." Many dogs live outside the circle of warmth and care that we extend to our pets. Quite a few of them are beyond even the minimum standards of decent treatment set by modern anticruelty laws.

Wild, Feral, and Stray Dogs

Several species of canids in South America, Asia, and Africa are called wild dogs. They are not members of the genus *Canis*, as dogs are. In fact, dogs are less closely related to these wild dog species than they are to wolves, jackals, and coyotes. Dogs that belong to the same species as domestic dogs but live in a wild or semi-wild way are not wild but feral. A feral animal is one that lives like a wild animal but that was once domesticated, or is descended from animals that were domesticated. The great majority of feral dogs, however, are descended from animals that have been feral for generations. Very few domestic dogs actually hunt, kill, and consume prey, but some feral dogs do so. Their prey generally consists of small creatures such as mice, lizards, and frogs, but some feral dogs prey on rabbits, cats, or chickens when they have the opportunity—usually around human settlements.

The ever-present village dogs of the developing world, called pariahs in India and pye-dogs in other parts of Asia, are mostly feral animals. Some of the dogs that scavenge in dumps by day, however, are associated with households to which they can return at night. Their "owners" may not feed them, but they are tolerated as watchdogs. Feral dogs also scrounge a living in the cities of the industrial world, snatching scraps from garbage

A FERAL DOG IN THAILAND. THROUGHOUT THE WORLD SUCH DOGS, DESCENDED FROM ANIMALS THAT WERE ONCE DOMESTIC, LIVE ON THE OUTSKIRTS OF HUMAN SOCIETY.

cans or getting by on handouts from sympathetic humans. Although occasionally a feral dog lives alone, such animals generally form loosely associated packs, with dominant and submissive members.

Australia has one of the world's most interesting and successful populations of feral dogs. They are called dingoes. Scientists used to think that dingoes were a species of wild dog, but in recent years they have identified dingoes as much closer relatives of the domestic dog. Some scientists call them *Canis*

DINGOES IN AUSTRALIA'S NORTHERN TERRITORY. ALTHOUGH DINGOES ARE NOW FERAL, SOME BIOLOGISTS THINK THAT THEY ARE THE CLOSEST LIVING LINKS TO THE FIRST DOMESTIC DOGS.

lupus dingo, which makes them, like dogs, a subspecies of wolf. Others call them *Canis familiaris dingo* or *Canis lupus familiaris dingo*, making them a subspecies of dog. Aside from the slippery and confusing question of names, dingoes are of special interest to scientists who study dogs and other canids. Experts now believe that dingoes are descended from dogs brought to Australia by people who migrated there thousands of years ago. Because Australia is an island, dingoes were isolated from other kinds of canids. They apparently soon became feral—in a sense, they were somehow "undomesticated"—and that is how they have remained. They have evolved so far back toward wildness that they are difficult to tame. Australian Aborigines today occasionally keep dingo pups as pets, but the animals always run away when they reach sexual maturity. Despite the dingo's feral way of life, some researchers think that it is the closest living example of what the first domestic dogs might have looked like, because it is descended directly from them without additional controlled breeding.

Strays are domestic dogs that have become lost, have run away, or have been abandoned. They are often hungry and confused; their behavior can range from dangerously aggressive to helpless. Unlike dogs that are born feral, strays seldom have good survival skills. A well-socialized stray may approach people, seeking to be adopted into a new "pack." Other strays die or end up in animal pounds. Those who manage to survive on their own may live to become part of the local feral dog community. Many people feel a strong impulse to help feral or stray dogs. Approaching such animals can be dangerous, however, because they may be infected with rabies or some other communicable disease. Most communities have some form of animal-control department that rounds up (and eventually destroys) wandering dogs, especially those that become pests.

SCAVENGING GARBAGE FROM A CONTAINER IN RUSSIA, THIS DOG MAY BE FERAL, BUT IT MAY ALSO BE A DOMESTIC DOG THAT HAS BECOME LOST OR BEEN CAST OFF BY ITS OWNERS. IF SO, IT MAY BE LUCKY ENOUGH TO FIND A NEW HOME. OR, IF IT MANAGES TO SURVIVE, IT AND ITS OFFSPRING WILL JOIN THE POPULATION OF FERAL DOGS.

Shelves upon shelves of books have been written about domestic dogs. There are hundreds of stories, both fact and fiction, about individual dogs' lives and adventures. Countless volumes offer advice on choosing, raising, training, and caring for dogs. The lore of dog breeds is enormous. Nearly every breed in existence has a body of literature devoted to it, with much discussion of that particular breed's traits, strengths, and weaknesses. Other books briefly list and describe hundreds of breeds. Still others recount the many things dogs do for people, such as search-and-rescue work, herding, and aiding the handicapped. There are stores that sell nothing but toys, beds, and other accessories for dogs. Events such as dog shows, sheepdog trials, and sled-dog races draw enthusiastic spectators. All these things are evidence of the great importance humans place on animals that share their lives.

People have found uses for dogs for thousands of years, but new uses keep emerging. Police use dogs as guards or to track fugitives. Dogs also assist law enforcement by performing tasks created by contemporary society—sniffing for illegal drugs and for bombs. For more than a century people have trained dogs to serve as guides for the blind. Today trainers also prepare dogs to aid people who are deaf or confined to wheelchairs—dogs can fetch and carry needed items and indicate when telephones or doorbells ring.

Perhaps the dog's greatest value, however, is as a companion. Scientific studies have shown that contact with tame, friendly animals has a positive effect on people—it lowers their blood pressure and reduces tension. An affectionate and well-socialized dog can give not just an emotional lift but also an immeasurable health benefit to the sick, the elderly, and the

DOGS HAVE BEEN HELPING HUMANS TEND OTHER ANIMALS FOR THOUSANDS OF YEARS. THIS BORDER COLLIE HERDING SHEEP IS PART OF AN ANCIENT TRADITION THAT STILL HAS A PLACE IN THE MODERN WORLD, ALTHOUGH MANY PEOPLE NOW KEEP HERDING DOGS AS PETS, WITHOUT THE HERDS.

depressed. In nursing homes for the elderly and in children's hospitals, the most eagerly awaited day of the week may be the day when handlers bring specially trained dogs for visits. Just stroking a dog or shaking its paw can be enough to brighten someone's day.

Dogs became the animals they are by a crude kind of genetic engineering, a long history of breeding and adapting

A VOLUNTEER FROM THE HUMANE SOCIETY INTRODUCES A PUPPY TO A NURSING-HOME RESIDENT. DOGS ARE NOT JUST MAN'S OLDEST ANIMAL FRIENDS—THEY ARE ALSO GOOD MEDICINE.

A DEPUTY SHERIFF AND HER CANINE PARTNER. MANY OF THOSE WHO LIVE AND WORK WITH DOGS SAY THAT THE BONDS OF AFFECTION, LOYALTY, AND TRUST THEY FORGE WITH THEIR ANIMALS ARE AS MEANINGFUL AS HUMAN RELATIONSHIPS. HUMANS HAVE SHAPED DOGS NOT ONLY TO MEET OUR NEEDS BUT ALSO TO EMBODY WHAT WE ADMIRE IN OUR OWN SPECIES.

that fitted them to our human needs. To those who appreciate the unique qualities of humankind's oldest animal partners, dogs are the best of companions. Sometimes, in their simplicity and loyalty, they even seem superior to people. The French poet Alphonse de Lamartine wrote in 1850, "The more I see of the representatives of the people, the more I admire my dogs."

Glossary

adapt—to change or develop in ways that aid survival

ancestral—having to do with lines of descent or earlier forms

breed—variety of animal within a species that has distinctive physical features

canid—member of the family Canidae, which includes wolves, jackals, foxes, coyotes, and wild and domestic dogs

canine—having to do with dogs

carnivore—animal that eats meat

chromosome—structure within a cell on which genes are arranged

conservation—action or movement aimed at saving or preserving wildlife or its habitat

domestication—taming; the process that turns a wild animal into one that humans raise, control, and use

evolve—to change over time; evolution is the process by which new species, or types of plants and animals, emerge from old ones

extinct—no longer existing; died out

genetic—having to do with genes, material made of DNA within the cells of living organisms. Genes carry information about inherited characteristics passed from parents to offspring

habitat—type of environment in which an animal lives

mammal—animal that nourishes its young with milk from its mammary glands. Dogs and humans are mammals, as are thousands of other animals

paleontologist—scientist who practices paleontology, the study of ancient and extinct life-forms, usually by examining fossil remains

prehistoric—before the invention of writing and the beginning of written history

Further Research

Books for Young People

Clutton-Brock, Juliet. *Dog*. New York: Dorling Kindersley, 2000.

Cole, Joanna. *A Dog's Body*. New York: Morrow, 1986.

Foster, Joanna. *Dogs Working for People*. Washington: National Geographic Society, 1972.

Glover, Harry. *The Book of Dogs*. New York: Viking Press, 1970.

Hughes, Dean. *Dog Detectives and Other Amazing Canines*. New York: Random House, 1994.

O'Neill, Amanda. *Dogs*. New York: Kingfisher, 1999.

Roalf, Peggy. *Dogs*. New York: Hyperion, 1993.

Silverstein, Alvin. *Dogs: All About Them*. New York: Lothrop, Lee & Shepard Books, 1986.

Singer, Marilyn. *A Dog's Gotta Do What a Dog's Gotta Do: Dogs at Work*. New York: Henry Holt, 2000.

Zeaman, John. *How the Wolf Became the Dog*. New York: Franklin Watts, 1998.

Videos

CBS/Fox Guide to Complete Dog Care. CBS/Fox Video, 1983.

Dog Obedience. Northstar Entertainment, 1998.

Puppy's First Year. Media West, 1996.

Those Wonderful Dogs: A National Geographic Special. Vestron Video, 1989.

Video Guide to Successful Dog Care. Maier Group Communications, 1989.

Web Sites

www.i-love-dogs.com A directory of hundreds of Web sites on everything from choosing a dog to jokes and stories about dogs.

www.akc.org The home page of the American Kennel Club, with information about purebred breeds and dog shows.

www.war-dogs.com This site tells the story of dogs who served with U.S. forces during the Vietnam War and the effort to build memorials to them.

www.dogsworldwide.com An online magazine and information exchange for dog lovers.

Bibliography

These books were especially useful to the author in researching this volume.

Coppinger, Raymond and Lorna Coppinger. *Dogs: A Startling New Understanding of Canine Origin, Behavior, and Evolution.* New York: Scribner, 2001.
A biologist and dogsled racer summarized theories and evidence about wolf-into-dog evolution, with discussions of how dogs fit into the concept of species and how humans have created dog breeds.

Coren, Stanley. *The Intelligence of Dogs: A Guide to the Thoughts, Emotions, and Inner Lives of Our Canine Companions.* New York: Bantam Books, 1995.
A scientist who specializes in studying the brain discusses dogs' intelligence and behavior.

Fiennes, Richard and Alice Fiennes. *A Natural History of Dogs.* Garden City, NY: Natural History Press, 1970.
Published for the American Museum of Natural History. An interesting look at the relationship between humans and dogs around the world since prehistoric times, although it does not contain the most up-to-date theories about dog origins.

Fogle, Bruce. *Know Your Dog: An Owner's Guide to Dog Behavior.* New York: Dorling Kindersley, 1992.
A veterinarian's easy-to-read accounts of aspects of canine life, from pack instincts to rearing puppies. Emphasis is on understanding dog behavior in order to live happily with dogs.

Hausman, Gerald and Loretta Hausman. *The Mythology of Dogs: Canine Legend and Lore through the Ages.* New York: St. Martin's Press, 1997.
Folklore and literary references organized by breed, covering sixty-seven kinds of dogs, from Afghans to Yorkshire terriers.

Reader's Digest Association. *The Reader's Digest Illustrated Book of Dogs.* Pleasantville, NY: Reader's Digest Association, 1982.
Includes a brief overview of dogs in history and art, descriptions of many breeds, and chapters on canine biology, reproduction, and care.

Thomas, Elizabeth Marshall. *The Hidden Life of Dogs*. Boston: Houghton Mifflin, 1993.
A look at canine psychology and behavior, with emphasis on how dogs interact with one another.

Verhoef-Verhallen, Esther J. *The Dog Encyclopedia*. Buffalo, NY: Firefly Books, 1996.
A handbook to the various categories of breeds, with brief descriptions of each breed's characteristics and many photographs.

Index

Page numbers for illustrations are in **boldface**.

About the Author

REBECCA STEFOFF has written many books on scientific and historical subjects for children and young adults. Among her books on animal life are *Horses, Bears,* and *Tigers* in Marshall Cavendish's *AnimalWays* series and the eighteen volumes of the *Living Things* series, also published by Marshall Cavendish. Stefoff lives in Portland, Oregon.